Original title:
Unsolved

Copyright © 2024 Swan Charm Publishing
All rights reserved.

Editor: Jessica Elisabeth Luik
Author: Sabrina Sarvik
ISBN HARDBACK: 978-9916-86-034-2
ISBN PAPERBACK: 978-9916-86-035-9

Elusive Truths

In shadows where secrets wane
Truths to the heart remain unseen
Elusive whispers call our name
Through the veil, they softly lean

We chase their fleeting glow
Through corridors of doubt and trust
Elusive, yet we toil to know
Journeys guided by the just

In quiet moments they appear
A glimpse, a spark, a fleeting gaze
Elusive truths we hold so dear
Through life's intricate, endless maze

When night and day converge as one
We ponder what is real, what dreams
Elusive truths by moon or sun
Ebb and flow like gentle streams

In hearts, in minds, they softly hide
Through time and space as wisdom grows
Elusive truths, our faithful guide
In life's dance, they ebb and flow

Mysterious Tales

In ancient tomes bound by years
Mysterious tales of yore we find
With ink and parchment, dreams and fears
Worlds within these pages confined

Through whispers carried by the breeze
The haunted lands and ghostly wails
In twilight's glow beneath the trees
Reside the most mysterious tales

Of love and loss, of joy and pain
Heralds of fates interwoven threads
Mysterious tales, forever remain
In minds, in hearts, with words unsaid

By candlelight, in hushed twilight
Echoes of ages long since gone
Mysterious tales come into sight
Till dawn breaks with a yawn

Through corridors of time and space
We travel with their guiding hands
Mysterious tales in their embrace
Reveal the heart of distant lands

Paths Not Taken

In forests deep, where shadows play,
Two trails diverge at break of day.
One well-trod, the other sparse,
Mysteries hidden in each arc.

Leaves rustle secrets, winds confide,
Choices linger where doubts reside.
Step by step, the heart debates,
Which way leads to fortune or fate?

Footprints etched in morning dew,
Mark the journey, old and new.
Paths not taken call and fade,
Echoes of a choice once made.

The Silent Code

In whispers soft, the language hides,
Between the words, where truth bides.
Unseen scripts, in dusk and dawn,
Silent codes, to ponder on.

Eyes can see but mind must read,
Intricate patterns that will lead.
Silent symbols, meanings bold,
Mysteries from the ancients told.

Listen close, to the silent song,
Decipher where the meanings throng.
In quiet realms, the secrets show,
Silent codes that one must know.

The Forgotten Thread

Threads of time unravel fast,
Memories of the distant past.
Woven tales, in fabric old,
Stars and dreams, stories untold.

Among the stitches, tales are spun,
Threads forgotten, by everyone.
Yet in the weave, the needle finds,
Patterns lost to wandering minds.

In silent looms of yesteryears,
Every thread has hidden spheres.
Forgotten strands may yet be found,
In tapestry of dreams profound.

Ciphers in the Fog

Mist rolls in, envelops sight,
Veiling whispers of the night.
Hidden codes, the fog enshrines,
Ciphers lost in ancient times.

Shapes emerge, then swiftly fade,
Ghostly forms in twilight shade.
Fog-bound secrets twine and swirl,
Wandering minds in mysteries furl.

Figures in the haze do gleam,
Fragments of a cryptic dream.
Decode the whispers in the fog,
Ciphers found in morning's smog.

Uncharted Minds

In caverns deep of thoughts untold,
Where whispers dance in veils of gold,
A realm unseen by eyes so blind,
The treasures lie in uncharted minds.

Embrace the tides of endless seas,
Within the heart, find precious keys,
Unlock the dreams in silent nights,
And chase the stars with boundless flights.

Through winding paths of doubt and fear,
Emerges hope, a voice so clear,
The journey vast, yet fate aligned,
For those who seek uncharted minds.

Cryptic Reflections

In mirrors' depths, where shadows play,
Lie cryptic truths, in shades of gray,
Reflections twist in endless maze,
Through time and space, in mirrored daze.

The visage seen, yet still unknown,
A soul reflected, yet alone,
With every glance, a new disguise,
Betrayed by eyes, the mirror lies.

Unravel threads of woven light,
Within the dark, the dawn so bright,
Cryptic reflections softly sing,
Of hidden wounds and healing spring.

Perplexing Horizons

At edges where the daylight wanes,
Horizons lure with boundless plains,
A mystic dance of dusk and dawn,
To seek the lands where dreams are drawn.

The sky ablaze in myriad hues,
With questions vast, and hidden clues,
Perplexing sights invite the mind,
To venture far, and answers find.

In shadows cast by setting sun,
New chapters start, the past is done,
Horizons stretch with silent grace,
Inviting all to find their place.

Unveiled Shadows

In realms where dusk and twilight meet,
The shadows weave an art so sweet,
Unveiled by night, the secrets show,
Within the dark, a mystic glow.

The tales untold by phantom light,
Awaken dreams in silent night,
A dance of whispers soft and low,
As shadows breathe in gentle flow.

In every shade, a story spun,
A tapestry by moon begun,
To those who seek with heart and mind,
Unveiled shadows, truth may find.

The Silent Enigma

In shadows deep, where secrets lie,
Mysterious forms in twilight shy,
A whisper trails through the breeze,
Unheard, unseen, with delicate ease.

Midnight's veil conceals unknown,
A silent riddle, carved in stone,
Silent stars in cosmic play,
Guard the enigmas of the day.

Through the echoes of a silent tune,
Mysteries dance beneath the moon,
Hallowed are the unseen threads,
Weaving stories the dark night spreads.

Lost in Time

Wanderer through the realms of past,
Echoes of moments, shadows cast,
Footprints fade on the sands,
Of an hourglass, slipping from hands.

Ancient tales in whispers float,
Histories penned on boats they bloat,
An endless quest to seek and find,
Lost fragments of a wandering mind.

In the corridors of days gone by,
Memories linger, never die,
Each tick, a stitch in fate's grand rhyme,
Forever lost, yet held in time.

A Riddle's Whisper

In a labyrinth of thoughts untold,
A riddle whispers, soft and bold,
Twisting paths where answers hide,
In shadows, where enigmas bide.

Questions linger in the night,
Dancing in the faint moonlight,
Mystic tones in every clue,
Hints of truths, in shades of blue.

Unraveling threads of cryptic lore,
To unlock secrets, evermore,
A journey deep, through mind's expanse,
Lost in the riddle's haunting dance.

Cryptic Night

Beneath the cover of the dark,
Where moonlight sketches a pale arc,
Cryptic forms in shadows play,
Guiding whispers in disarray.

Stars like cryptographs align,
To reveal truths so serpentine,
Symbolic tales in night's deep hue,
Shapes of dreams in silent view.

A symphony of hidden sights,
Translated through the cryptic nights,
Every moment, a veiled decree,
Whispering secrets to those who see.

Abyss of Queries

In the darkened pit of thought, we dwell
Mysteries wrapped in shadows' veil
We seek the truth in whispered spells
Yet answers float just beyond the pale

What lies beneath the twilight's cloak?
Questions spark, igniting minds
Reason struggles, logic chokes
In the labyrinth where clarity hides

Voices echo, unheard, unseen
Through endless corridors of doubt
We chase reflections, ne'er serene
In the silent shadows, we scout

Ephemeral threads of wisdom weave
Patterns lost in the void of night
In the abyss, we still believe
That questions guide us towards the light

The Unheard Story

In whispers soft, the tale unfolds
Through windswept fields and ancient scripts
A story lost, in shadows holds
Its verses dance on silent lips

Unseen by eyes, the journey's mark
Etched in time's relentless flow
An age-old song sung in the dark
By voices no one seems to know

A saga carved in grains of sand
Its heroes fade beneath the waves
Where memories touch the dream-laden land
And echoes rise from unmarked graves

Binding threads of fate's cruel jest
With hope that lingers in the dust
An unheard story, heart's true quest
To honor life and love, we trust

Ghosts of the Unknown

In twilight's grasp, the specters glide
Unseen phantoms of the unseen past
They wander where our secrets hide
In shadows where the dreams must last

Their whispers chill the night-bound air
Murmurs of lives we never knew
In vacant rooms, their souls despair
For stories left untold and true

Lost in the echoes of the mind
They drift through time's eternal seam
Where memories and moments bind
Like fragments of a broken dream

Beneath the moon's reflective light
They trace the paths we've yet to tread
Ghosts of the unknown, in their plight
Haunt the realms of the silent dead

Hidden Narratives

In pages worn by history's grace
Lurk tales untold beneath the ink
In shadows' depth, they find their place
Where secrets lie, and thoughts do sink

Veiled stories whisper in the dark
Of lives entwined with fate's cruel hand
Unraveled truths leave their mark
In silences we misunderstand

Each hidden narrative, a thread
Woven tight through fabric's span
Binding voices of the dead
To journeys mapped by unseen plan

In undisclosed, the heart does yearn
For mysteries wrapped in books' embrace
With each locked tale, new truths discern
The hidden narratives we trace

Questions in the Wind

In fields where shadows play
The whispers never end
Leaves rustle in disarray
With secrets they defend

What truths the breezes hide
In their uncertain song
Unknown, the answers bide
Where mysteries belong

Soft murmurs call my name
Through canopies of green
A tantalizing flame
Of worlds yet unseen

Do questions ever cease?
Or linger in the air?
The wind denies me peace
Still asking, unaware

An ancient riddle's breath
Through time and space it weaves
A tale of life and death
Like whispers on the leaves

The Missing Clue

A puzzle left unsolved
In pages dust does keep
Mysteries bit revolved
In shadows dark and deep

The search was long and wide
No answer to be found
Where did the secret hide?
In places so profound

Through corridors of time
I walked, my lantern dim
The echoes sang in rhyme
Of whispers cold and grim

Each piece I sought to frame
Eluded till the dawn
An endless, silent game
Resuming at each yawn

A fragment held in hand
Yet one more truth's aloof
The missing clue demands
Unwavering pursuit

Elusive Patterns

Patterns on the sand
Shift beneath the tide
Drawn by nature's hand
In beauty they confide

A tapestry unseen
By those who dare not look
In threads of evergreen
As written in a book

Each wave a brush's stroke
On canvas wide and gray
An artist's words evoked
In water and in spray

I chase the lines askew
They lead me ever far
Their meaning still askew
Like light from a distant star

Elusive is the plot
In nature's grand design
A story seldom caught
Yet endlessly divine

Fragments of the Unknown

Pieces scattered wide
Across a realm untamed
Fragments of the tide
In chaos yet unnamed

From dreams they seem to rise
Soft glimpses of the veil
Tales of starry skies
And ships without a sail

Elusive to the mind
Yet present in the dark
A quest all undefined
To chase a fleeting spark

Unknown, they drift and blend
Into the silent night
Each fragment a new end
Or maybe morning's light

What secrets do they hold?
These shards of cosmic lore
In silence they unfold
A mystery to explore

Uncharted Waters

Beneath the waves, secrets lie
In depths where shadows sigh
No compass guides the way
To lands where legends play

Voyagers dream of distant shores
A place where time ignores
The siren songs, they softly call
Through oceans' endless sprawl

The moonlight dances on the sea
In silvery mystery
Uncharted waters, bold and vast
Where futures forge from past

Strangers' tales and whispered lore
Of worlds we've yet explored
Guide me through this liquid night
To find a hidden light

The stars above reflect below
As gentle breezes blow
In search of paths we've never crossed
Where dreams are never lost

Puzzling Silhouettes

In twilight's quiet, shadows play
With forms that shift and sway
A puzzle etched in evening's hues
Where light and darkness fuse

Each silhouette a story hides
Of secrets, undefined
In whispered tones, they softly speak
Of answers we all seek

The night becomes a canvas vast
With mysteries that last
Each shadow forms a piece anew
In a tapestry of blue

Beneath the moon's attentive gaze
The world becomes a maze
Of puzzling shapes and shades unseen
Where nothing's as it seems

In darkness, we find shapes emerge
From shadows' quiet surge
Their cryptic dance, a silent quest
In shadows, truth does rest

The Secret Maze

Each twist and turn conceals a clue
In labyrinths of dew
Where whispers guide uncertain ways
Through endless nights and days

The hedges hide a path untrue
A riddle made of two
Each branch a choice, each step a test
Toward a hidden quest

The walls that close and lead astray
Challenge with their play
Within the maze, a secret sleeps
In shadows, deep it keeps

The stars above give gentle light
In maze's darkened night
A journey through the tangled web
Where hopes are softly fed

At heart of maze, the secrets lie
Beneath the midnight sky
To find the way, one must be brave
And see beyond the grave

Mystic Charades

In theater of dreams they play
Where shadows slip away
A masquerade in twilight's gleam
Of actors' unseen scheme

The mystic dance of hidden truths
In whispers, dreams are sleuths
Each gesture holds a secret part
Of life's enraptured art

Disguised in masks of night they move
With steps they can't disprove
The actors bow to silent skies
In moonlit charades wise

A charade of mystic lore untold
Where stories soft unfold
In riddles wrapped in twilight's mist
By shadows, gently kissed

The curtain falls on secret stage
Where dreams and night engage
In charades of mystic, silent grace
Where truth and dreams embrace

Labyrinth of Questions

Through corridors of doubt we tread,
With echoes of the past ahead.
Corners turn and pathways wind,
Seeking truths we hope to find.

A whisper here, a shadow cast,
Navigating the questions vast.
No map to guide, no stars align,
Just endless loops of twisting vine.

The heart inquires, the mind reflects,
Destiny's maze, so indirect.
Footsteps falter, souls entwine,
In this labyrinth, we search and pine.

Each doorway leads to realms unknown,
A tapestry of time has shown.
Threads of wonder, threads of fear,
In this maze, the answers near.

Yet on we go, through paths unclear,
With every step the end draws near.
A labyrinth of questions wrought,
In each unfold a deeper thought.

Secrets Left Behind

Whispers carried by the breeze,
Silent tales among the trees.
Shadows dance in moonlit light,
Secrets hidden from our sight.

An echo of a distant past,
Memories that everlast.
Locked away in rooms of mind,
Fragments of what's left behind.

A diary lost, a letter torn,
Voices of the forlorn.
Ghosts of stories left unread,
Linger where the words have bled.

The ocean's waves, the mountains' crest,
Holding secrets close to chest.
Ancient whispers, winds that bind,
Echo secrets left behind.

Treasures buried, lips that sealed,
Moments that were never healed.
In the quiet of the mind,
Lay the secrets left behind.

The Shadow's Riddle

In twilight's hush, a riddle spins,
A shadow moves, the tale begins.
Elusive as the morning mist,
A mystery no light can twist.

It whispers through the night so deep,
In secrets only dark can keep.
An enigma that does not cease,
A puzzle piece, elusive peace.

The shadow dances, slips away,
A fleeting glance, a phantom play.
Within its grasp the answers hide,
A riddle with no true abide.

Fragmented clues in shadows cast,
Prints of time that seem to last.
A chase that circles, never ends,
Until the shadow's truth descends.

In every corner, every light,
The shadow holds its grasp so tight.
A riddle spun in dark array,
The shadow's secret for all who stray.

A Mystery Unspooled

Threads of fate in stories told,
Woven from some loom of old.
Each minute draws a line so fine,
Within the weave, a tale divine.

A clock unwinds, seconds flee,
Moments turn to memory.
Cast upon the tapestry,
Mystery unspools so free.

Whispers from the grains of sand,
Messages in greying strands.
Unravel what was tightly wound,
Secrets lost, and then they're found.

Every turn, a twist reveals,
Intricate, the story seals.
In the loom of life's grand spool,
Mysteries unwind and rule.

From end to end, a narrative,
A story's depths, we seem to live.
In each strand, the world uncooled,
Forever spins, a mystery unspooled.

Arcane Whispers

In the night's embrace, secrets roam
Carried by winds that softly moan
Echoes of ages, shadows dense
Veiling truths in vague pretense

Mysterious murmurs through the trees
Ancestral voices on the breeze
Shrouded paths that time conceals
Revealed in whispers, truths unsealed

Glimmering stars light the unknown
Safeguarding tales the dark has sown
Through ethereal realms we drift
Seeking keys, the fog to lift

Cryptic symbols etched in stone
Guarding realms to men unknown
In twilight's glow, the veil thins
Arcane whispers cease, night begins

Forgotten Signals

Faint pulses from a distant shore
Memories lost, now something more
Waves of time, in silence break
Ancient truths, from sleep awake

Flickers of light, once bright and pure
Fractured visions, blurred, obscure
Signposts from an age gone by
Calling out, a silence cry

Unraveled codes of yesteryears
Whispers that fall on silent ears
River of dreams, where shadows lie
Tracing secrets, edges nigh

Spectral hands, in twilight write
Messages in endless night
Through void's abyss, signals yearn
To be known, and thus return

Unknown Sentinels

Guardians of the unseen fold
Silent watchers, stories untold
Vigil keepers, shadows thin
Ancient eyes with secrets pinned

Stars align in cryptic forms
Guiding us through countless storms
Eternal watch, in silence cast
Unknown sentinels of the past

Mountains rise to touch the sky
Timeless whispers in their sigh
Whispered oaths in shadow's breath
Sentinels, defying death

Invisible lines that cross our fates
Unseen guardians at our gates
Through the void, their visions roam
Unknown sentinels, leading home

Masquerade of Time

In masquerade, time dons a mask
Weaving tales from dusk till dawn
Moments pass, like fleeting gleams
In the dance of ancient dreams

Faces change, as seasons glide
Mysteries in shadows hide
Whispers of the years unwound
In the masquerade's soft sound

Eternal waltz, through time's vast hall
Phantom echoes, rise and fall
Life's charade, a fleeting mime
Played within the hands of time

Veils of midnight, thin and frail
Stories told in moonlight's trail
Unraveled threads, a grand design
In the masquerade, we intertwine

Secrets in Starlight

Beneath the canopy of night,
Soft whispers trace the sky.
In every glimmer, hope takes flight,
As dreams and secrets lie.

The stars, with languages unknown,
Spin tales of ancient lore.
Within their twinkle softly shown,
Are wishes, evermore.

The midnight breeze carries afar,
Chants to the heavens call.
Mysteries in each distant star,
Where shadows gently fall.

A dance of light in deepest dark,
Unveils the hidden trail.
Each secret leaves a tiny mark,
In cosmos' silent veil.

So gaze upon the silent sea,
Where starlight secrets wend.
In twilight's hush, our dreams run free,
Until night's gentle end.

Cryptic Journeys

Through winding paths in twilight's hold,
Where shadows weave their spell.
A journey's cryptic tale unfolds,
In whispers none can tell.

Each step unlocks a boundless reach,
To realms both near and far.
With every turn, untamed they teach,
In silence, like a star.

The cryptic message rides the wind,
In echoes, true yet faint.
To understand is to rescind,
Each fear, each soft complaint.

Within these trails, an ancient guide,
Attend in shadows' bend.
Their cryptic secrets to confide,
To those who seek and mend.

Through journeys veiled in mystic grey,
Where twilight shades align.
The cryptic path of night and day,
Unfolds its grand design.

Hushed Intervals

In moments where the silence speaks,
    And time itself stands still.
The hushed intervals softly peek,
    With whispers pure and chill.

Amid the world's relentless hum,
    A pause, so brief yet clear.
In hushed intervals, thoughts become
    The echoes we hold dear.

Each breath, a tether to the soul,
    Within the silent trace.
The inner whispers gently roll,
    In intervals of grace.

Hushed intervals, they carve the way,
    Through life's unending maze.
A fleeting moment's soft relay,
    In time's eternal glaze.

So cherish quiet's tender hug,
As shadows warmly creep.
For in these intervals, we tug
The heartstrings that we keep.

Veiled Verses

In ancient tomes of hidden prose,
The veiled verses lie.
Through cryptic lines, a mystery grows,
Beneath the reader's eye.

Each word a shadow, softly cast,
Upon the parchment rare.
In veiled verses, tales have passed,
On whispers through the air.

Encrypted in the silken ink,
The secrets of a time.
Where stories flow beyond the brink,
In rhythm and in rhyme.

The veiled verses hide their song,
In languages of old.
Yet, in their cadence, clear and strong,
The hidden truths unfold.

So reach within the shadow's weave,
And seek the mystic lore.
For in the veiled verses, believe,
Lies knowledge to explore.

Enigmatic Glows

Beneath the moons mysterious sway,
Where shadows dance, and silence stays.
A luminescent secret flows,
In cryptic, radiant, evening shows.

Stars whisper tales we scarcely know,
Gleams hint at truths that never show.
In twilight's grip, enigmas grow,
And through the dusk, the answers flow.

Veil the world in shrouded light,
Where specters weave through darkest night.
Elusive glimmers in the gloam,
Guide us toward a hidden home.

Echoes of an ancient lore,
Embers glow on distant shore.
To twilight's call, we truly bow,
Embracing night's enigma now.

Mysteries in the winds are sown,
By galaxies in twilight thrown.
With each reveal, yet more unknown,
In endless search of truths unshown.

Whispers of the Abyss

In the depths where darkness waits,
Eternal void at ancient gates.
Whispers curl through fathom's deep,
Secrets buried, shadows keep.

Silence reigns where light once played,
Echoes of the lost displayed.
Abyss speaks with muffled cries,
Hidden truths in dark disguise.

Tides of time in stillness drift,
Whispers rise on currents swift.
Invisible, the depths' refrain,
Tales of sorrow, endless pain.

Beneath the waves, a hidden voice,
In oblivion, seeks no choice.
Blanketed in somber shroud,
Lost amid the darkness' cloud.

In the chasm, whispers soar,
Beckoning to night's dark lore.
Abyssal secrets, softly hissed,
In darkness, we exist.

Lost Frequencies

In the silence, currents hum,
Frequencies of worlds become.
Lost to time, yet ever near,
Mystic tones we barely hear.

Walls of sound, an unseen sea,
Vibrations echo ceaselessly.
In a void where echoes reign,
Memory's song, a soft refrain.

Through the ether's secret song,
Lost frequencies roam along.
Connection to a distant past,
Echoing through shadows cast.

Hidden waves in realms unseen,
Whisper truths in soft, serene.
In the space where silence wings,
Lost in time, the echo sings.

Tune your soul to hidden streams,
Catch the song within your dreams.
In the heartbeat, softly flows,
Frequencies the cosmos knows.

Baffling Melodies

In twilight's grasp, the melodies weave,
Sounds that mystify and deceive.
Tunes of shadows, notes of night,
Haunting whispers out of sight.

Unfamiliar rhythms blend,
Passages that have no end.
Melodies of dreams untold,
Mysteries within them hold.

Harmonics twist through dusky air,
Baffling, perplexing, rare.
Ancient songs from times of old,
Resonate, their tales unfold.

Chords that stir the echoes deep,
In their wake, the spirits leap.
Through the veil of night they drift,
Baffling tunes, a cryptic gift.

Incomprehensible refrain,
Woven through the shadows' gain.
Melodies that leave us dazed,
Lost in twilight's foggy maze.

Eclipsed Memoirs

In shadows where the memories lie,
A whispered name begins to fade,
Under a moonless, silent sky,
Their echoes lost in twilight's glade.

Pages turned by hands unseen,
Words dissolve in dusk's embrace,
Ephemeral as a forgotten dream,
The heart's old stories leave no trace.

Embers of the past arise,
Only to vanish in the haze,
Caught between the truths and lies,
Lost in that eternal daze.

The night absorbs their quiet pleas,
Where even stars dare not to pry,
In the darkness, no one sees,
The memories whispered, then they die.

The Dark Labyrinth

Twisting corridors of night,
Echoes of the lost resound,
In every corner hides a fright,
Where shadows darken all around.

A maze of whispers, cold and deep,
Where light can hardly find its way,
Secrets buried in the keep,
Guarded by the night and day.

Search for the path, though none is clear,
In the silence of the mind,
Haunted by a constant fear,
Of more than you could ever find.

Yet forward still, you must proceed,
Through the realms of darkened thought,
For in the labyrinth, you'll need,
To face the battles you have fought.

Echoes in Silence

Soft as snowflakes in the dusk,
Words unspoken fill the air,
In the shadows, memories husk,
Of dreams that never could repair.

And in the stillness, whispers glide,
Across the chasm of the past,
Where hopes and fears slowly collide,
In echoes silence can't outlast.

Lonely voices, ghostly thin,
Linger where the heart once stayed,
In the quiet, deep within,
They haunt the spaces dreams have made.

Though silence reigns, it cannot quell,
The echoes of what might have been,
For in the silence, they still dwell,
Until the day they're born again.

The Unknown Pages

In a book without a name,
Written words unseen by eyes,
Lies a tale without acclaim,
Where every truth in silence lies.

Chapters filled with might-have-beens,
Stories etched in unseen ink,
In the margins, every sin,
Lost in thoughts too deep to think.

The unknown pages, daunting, stark,
Hold the might of what's unseen,
In the glow of fading spark,
Lie the ghosts of dreams serene.

To read these pages is to find,
Mysteries that sleep in dust,
Every line a twist of mind,
Every tale a fragile trust.

Hushed Shadows

Amidst the twilight's gentle glow,
Hushed shadows quietly bestow,
A whisper of the night's embrace,
Soft secrets in a darkened space.

Silent murmurs fill the night,
As dreams take flight, a mystic sight,
Veils of darkness softly cling,
Encasing whispers that they bring.

Stars above in silent dance,
Casting spells of night's romance,
Through the stillness, shadows weave,
Tales of old, they quietly leave.

As the moonlight gently fades,
In the hushed and quiet glades,
Shadows fade, the morning wakes,
Silent mysteries, dawn breaks.

In the calm of night's retreat,
Past and present softly meet,
Time's concealed yet tender flow,
Hushed shadows guide where dreams go.

Invisible Strings

Beneath the surface, ties unseen,
Invisible strings in life's grand scheme,
Binding hearts across the way,
In a silent, seamless sway.

Through the currents of the air,
Connections form a lattice rare,
Unknown forces, strong yet thin,
Weaving souls from deep within.

In the spaces, void and vast,
Echoes of the future and the past,
Lines that bind, yet can't be seen,
Threads of fate within us glean.

Drawn together by the pull,
Of energies both sharp and dull,
These unseen threads, both lost and found,
Tie us to the world around.

Mysteries of what life brings,
Guided by these hidden strings,
In the silence, we are tied,
By threads that bind us, far and wide.

Eccentric Rhythms

Underneath a moonlit sky,
Eccentric rhythms sway and fly,
A dance of stars in cosmic play,
In intricate and wild array.

Flashes of an errant beat,
Echoes form a grand retreat,
Time itself dissolves and twirls,
In the night's unfolding whirls.

Nature's pulse, an untamed song,
In night's embrace, it hums along,
Patterns shift and intertwine,
In rhythms odd, yet so divine.

Chaos holds a beauty rare,
Surreal sounds that fill the air,
With each note, a fleeting sight,
In this dance of pure delight.

Eccentric is the way they flow,
As night and stars put on their show,
Through the twilight's endless stream,
In rhythms strange, we dare to dream.

Twilight Paradox

In the twilight's soft embrace,
Lies a paradox, time's gentle chase,
Day's end and night's sweet birth,
A fleeting bridge 'twixt heaven and earth.

Dusky hues of gold and grey,
Heralding the close of day,
Yet within their fading light,
A promise of the coming night.

In the twilight's pensive glow,
Veiled truths begin to show,
Mysteries of time unwind,
Shadows of the future left behind.

A balance in the twilight's sheen,
Where past and present lie between,
Infinite in its brief delay,
Night encroaches on the day.

In this temporal, gentle flux,
Lies the twilight's paradox,
A fleeting moment, still and bright,
Caught between the day and night.

Beyond the Curtain

Whispers in twilight's embrace,
Secrets hidden from the light,
Behind the veil, a sacred place,
   Where dreams take flight.

A world unknown, yet so near,
Boundaries blurred by the night,
Step beyond without fear,
   Into realms of pure delight.

Shadows dance with tender grace,
   Mysteries softly unveiled,
   Eyes closed, see the trace,
Of where souls have sailed.

Beyond the curtain's silken flow,
   Truths and fantasies twine,
Where only the brave may go,
   To find what's truly divine.

Mystical Allure

Moonlight whispers on the sea,
Stars like lanterns in the sky,
Nature's endless symphony,
Invokes a gentle sigh.

Mysteries with every breeze,
Secrets tangled in the air,
Captured by the silent trees,
As night lays its snare.

Glowing orbs in midnight streams,
Flickering through the pines,
Guardians of forgotten dreams,
They watch for ancient signs.

In the hush of twilight's glow,
Magic lingers pure,
Inviting hearts to freely flow,
In mystical allure.

Inexplicable Silence

Quiet fills the empty room,
Deafening in its might,
Whispered memories in the gloom,
Echo through the night.

Words unspoken, hearts entwined,
In stillness, we confide,
The silence of a thoughtful mind,
Where secrets gently hide.

Transcendent peace or aching loss,
A silence hard to bear,
A crossroad we both come across,
In moments we can't share.

Inexplicable, yet profound,
This silence speaks to me,
In every pause, a truth is found,
In its tranquil sea.

Labyrinth of Dreams

Twisting paths of moonlit haze,
Through corridors of night,
We wander in a mystic daze,
Beyond the edge of sight.

Lost in realms of fantasy,
Where thoughts become entwined,
A dance with our own sanity,
In the caverns of the mind.

Echoes of forgotten lore,
Softly call our name,
In the maze, we seek for more,
Shadows flicker like a flame.

Labyrinthine tales unfold,
In this sacred dreamer's lair,
Every twist a secret told,
In the magic of the air.

The Unanswered Call

In twilight's soft and somber glow,
A whisper threads the evening air,
An echo from the world below,
A call unanswered, lost somewhere.

The stars align, a silent choir,
Their light a guide through shadows deep,
Yet through this void, the heart's desire,
Remains a mystery we keep.

The wind it sings a mournful song,
Of dreams that never found their course,
Of every right that turned to wrong,
Beneath the night's relentless force.

And in the hush where time stands still,
A fleeting moment seems to fall,
A spark that no one sees until,
It's gone—the unanswered call.

Embrace the night, embrace the light,
For both will guide you through the hall,
And when the dawn awakens bright,
Perhaps you'll hear that distant call.

Shades of Ambiguity

In twilight's veil of gray and blue,
Where certainty cannot reside,
A realm where countless dreams accrue,
And shifting shadows softly bide.

The hues between the black and white,
Where truth and lies converge in dance,
In shades of ambiguity's light,
Illusions twist with fine romance.

The path ahead, it twists and wanes,
With choices cloaked in veiled disguise,
Yet through the clouds and gentle rains,
We learn to see with inner eyes.

For clarity is oft a muse,
One dressed in robes of mystery,
And ambiguity's gentle hues,
Create our life's rich tapestry.

In spaces where shadows blend and play,
Our hearts discern what eyes cannot,
Embrace the gray, accept the sway,
In ambiguity, truth is sought.

Hidden Truths

Beneath the earth, where roots entwine,
In depths where secrets lie concealed,
Exist hidden truths, both dark and fine,
In shadows where past wounds are healed.

Whispers of old through ancient stones,
The voices of the past resound,
In murmurs soft, the world atones,
For truths that time has tightly bound.

Within the heart, a maze unfolds,
Of buried fears and silent cries,
Through labyrinths of stories told,
Hidden truths await our eyes.

Look deep within, where shadows cease,
Beyond the masks we often wear,
In quietude, our souls find peace,
And hidden truths lay bare with care.

As daylight breaks the night's long fast,
Illuminates what once was lost,
The hidden truths emerge at last,
And bid us face them, free of cost.

Veiled Mysteries

The moonlight casts a silver sheen,
Upon the world's enshrouded guise,
Veiled mysteries in places unseen,
Unfold before our wondering eyes.

The night breathes secrets through the air,
In whispers soft, both old and new,
Each starlit spark, a hidden lair,
Of stories waiting to accrue.

Beyond the veil, where shadows play,
A tapestry of dreams unfurls,
In twilight's grip, both night and day,
Hold mysteries like precious pearls.

In silence, truths and lies collide,
Crafting tales we yearn to know,
Veiled mysteries in darkness hide,
Yet through our hearts, their whispers flow.

Embrace the unknown paths ahead,
For there, life's magic blooms and grows,
In veiled mysteries gently spread,
Lie wonders only courage shows.

Through the Veil

Beyond the misty curtain,
Lies worlds yet unseen.
Soft whispers call through twilight,
Voices of what has been.

Past shadows dance in silence,
A spectral waltz of grace.
Time's tapestry unravels,
Revealing every face.

In realms where dreams take flight,
And thoughts can cast their spell.
We find truths deeply hidden,
In places we not dwell.

Stars shiver in the distance,
Orbs of ancient lore.
Guiding us through darkness,
To secret unknown shores.

Through the veil we journey,
With hearts that dare to seek.
Embracing all that's mystic,
In moments dire and bleak.

Mysteries of the Heart

In chambers dark and silent,
Where emotions softly sleep.
Lies secrets always guarded,
Promises we keep.

A labyrinth of feeling,
Twists and turns uncharted.
Desires whispered lightly,
Into hearts tender-hearted.

Love's flame burns eternal,
In the shadows deep.
Passions like a tempest,
In laughter and in weep.

The heart speaks its own language,
Of joy and hidden sorrow.
Each beat a subtle story,
Of today, and of tomorrow.

Dive into its echoes,
Where mysteries are spun.
In the heart's vast ocean,
True wonderments are won.

Echoes of the Unknown

In the silence of the midnight,
Where shadows softly creep.
Echoes of the unknown,
From the depths they seep.

Waves of ancient voices,
Across time they call.
Stories left untold,
In whispers they enthrall.

The wind it sings of secrets,
In languages untaught.
Leaving us to ponder,
The mysteries they've brought.

Moonlight paints a portrait,
On a canvas dark and wide.
Showing us reflections,
Of the worlds that hide inside.

Tune your ear to listen,
To the songs of long ago.
In echoes of the unknown,
Truths begin to show.

Shadows in the Night

When twilight folds its curtains,
And day gives way to night.
Shadows drape like velvet,
In the absence of light.

The moon casts ghostly figures,
On walls of ancient stone.
Shadows dance in silence,
Their secrets left unknown.

A symphony of darkness,
Plays a nocturnal tune.
Conducted by the starlight,
Beneath the watchful moon.

Each secret place they wander,
Each corner that they find.
Holds stories of the timeless,
In the recesses of the mind.

So walk with careful footsteps,
In the stillness of the dark.
Where shadows in the night,
Leave their fleeting mark.

Silent Whispers

In the hush of twilight's grace,
Where shadows softly trace,
Lies a world of silent whispers,
Oft hidden from our gaze.

Among the trees and ancient groves,
Secrets of the heart unspool,
Carried by a gentle breeze,
In mystic, muted droves.

Soft murmurs fill the starlit skies,
As moonlight tenderly replies,
To the voice of quiet yearning,
In whispered lullabies.

In the quiet of the night,
Where dreams and wishes intertwine,
The whispers call us to belong,
In silence, oh so fine.

Enigmatic Paths

Winding roads of mystery,
Through woods and twilight's symphony,
Lead us on through realms unknown,
To destiny's soft plea.

Veiled in mist, the journey starts,
A trail through enigmatic arts,
Each step a riddle to unfold,
As hearts and minds become the charts.

Stars align to light the way,
Through night and uncertain day,
Guided by an unseen thread,
In faith, we dare to stray.

Though paths may twist and fate may play,
With shadows that both gleam and sway,
We walk these roads with hope held high,
To find our truth, come what may.

Secrets in Time

In the echoes of the past,
Where ancient stories last,
Lie the secrets kept by time,
In shadows long to cast.

Whispers from a bygone age,
Hidden within history's page,
Speak of love, of loss, and dreams,
And wisdom of a sage.

Through the sands that gently fall,
In time's unwavering thrall,
Mysteries concealed unveil,
Both monumental and small.

Among the ruins old and grand,
With time's caress in hand,
The secrets wait to be revealed,
In timeless vast expanse.

Ciphers in the Wind

Messages in breeze's flight,
Dancing in the moon's soft light,
Ciphers carried on the air,
With secrets hidden from our sight.

Leaves whisper secrets from the trees,
Enigmas in the passing breeze,
Words unspoken, tales untold,
In the wind's mysterious ease.

From distant lands and far-off dreams,
Ciphers float on silent streams,
To those who listen with their hearts,
The wind's soft murmur gleams.

In every gust, a story spun,
In every breeze, a race begun,
To decode the wind's soft song,
And find the truth in one.

Untold Epilogues

Beneath the leaves of autumn's gentle sway,
Where whispers of the past forever stay,
Forgotten tales in shadows often play,
The epilogues that time can't keep at bay.

In moonlit fields, where dreams and night converge,
Silent echoes of old stories surge,
Unfinished lines on time's unraveling verge,
In timeless loops eternally emerge.

The parchment of the sky in ink so dark,
Bears the traces of a fading spark,
Unwritten chapters, weary souls embark,
Upon the paths where destinies embark.

Silent stars compose forgotten lines,
Distant memories that time defines,
In cosmic libraries where time aligns,
Books of life where every vow entwines.

And in the silence of the twilight's hush,
Where ancient winds through timeless valleys rush,
Epilogues whisper in a gentle hush,
That through the ages hearts will ever brush.

Hushed Confessions

Beneath the cloak of starlit, velvet night,
The secrets of our hearts take silent flight,
In whispered tones we dare to bring to light,
Confessions left in shadows, out of sight.

Soft murmurs weave through sighs of evening air,
Revealing truths we're too afraid to bear,
In quiet moments when the world's not there,
We lay our souls with delicate care.

Beneath the moon's soft gaze, our hearts unfold,
Love's hidden tales in secret, meek and bold,
The treasures of our spirits, rich as gold,
In hushed confessions, tenderly retold.

The night, a keeper of our veiled desires,
To whom we whisper all that truth inspires,
Within its silent embrace, as old as sires,
Our hopes and dreams rekindle like fires.

Come close and let the night absorb our fears,
In hushed confessions, lost to time and years,
The moonlight dries our softly falling tears,
As we unveil our souls, and silence cheers.

Chasing Echoes

Across the valleys, through the hills so wide,
Where shadows of old memories reside,
We chase echoes on the winds that ride,
Lost voices that time cannot abide.

In caverns deep where whispers gently weep,
And secrets of the earth in silence keep,
The echoes of the past begin to seep,
Through every dream that carries us to sleep.

Mountains tall, they cradle sounds of yore,
Ancient songs that time could not ignore,
As we pursue, our hearts begin to soar,
Along the paths where echoes evermore.

The rivers speak in murmured, hushed refrain,
Of times long past, of joy and subtle pain,
In chasing echoes, all that does remain,
Are traces of eternity's sweet strain.

Through twilight's veil, we wander close and far,
Guided by a dimly glowing star,
Chasing echoes, memories are ajar,
In haunting chords, as endless as they are.

Undefined Destinies

In the spaces where our dreams collide,
Lies the path we venture on, untried,
Undefined destinies, together, side by side,
We navigate the currents, life's vast tide.

The future is a canvas, white and pure,
With every step, our vision shall ensure,
That every stroke of fate we must endure,
Creates a masterpiece, our hearts assure.

The crossroads of tomorrow stand in wait,
With every choice we make, we elevate,
Undefined destinies we contemplate,
The mysteries of life we navigate.

Through starry nights and dusks of every hue,
We walk the journey, old yet ever new,
Undefined destinies we will pursue,
With open hearts and spirits bold, and true.

In the whispers of the wind's sweet breath,
Lie promises of life beyond mere death,
Undefined destinies with every step,
We write our stories with each fleeting breath.

The Phantom's Secret

In shadows deep, where phantoms roam,
A secret kept beneath the gloam.
Whispers faint, of truths untold,
A mystery woven, eons old.

Through silent halls, with footsteps light,
The phantom keeps its secret tight.
A flicker here, a shadow there,
Guarding secrets, thin as air.

In misted veil, from moonlit skies,
A tale of whispers softly lies.
Ephemeral, the secret's song,
Echoes faintly, all night long.

Waiting for the dawn to break,
For someone brave the steps to take.
A secret shared, a burden freed,
The phantom's heart, its silent creed.

Yet still, it lingers, bound to keep,
A vow of silence, dark and deep.
The phantom's secret, shadows bound,
In twilight's hold, forever found.

Whispers of the Past

In ancient winds, where whispers call,
The past returns, a spectral thrall.
Histories tread in echoes clear,
Whispers of the past draw near.

Through worn-out tales in faded ink,
Forgotten truths begin to sink.
In silent nights, the past revives,
Its whispered breath in darkness thrives.

Old memories, like fleeting dreams,
Flow through time's relentless streams.
In shadows cast, they linger free,
Whispers of what used to be.

Beneath the stars, in quiet skies,
The past unveils its hidden ties.
A tapestry of lives once led,
Whispers from the long gone dead.

As dawn approaches, shadows fade,
The whispers too will soon be staid.
But echoes leave a lasting trace,
Of whispers past, in time and space.

The Hidden Puzzle

In cryptic marks, where shadows play,
Lies a puzzle night and day.
An enigma bound by secret code,
A hidden path where few have strode.

Pieces scattered, far and wide,
In silent clues and whispers tied.
A journey through the veiled and sly,
The hidden puzzle calls your eye.

With every step and every turn,
New mysteries, your mind to churn.
Unlock the secrets, piece by piece,
For the hidden puzzle's sweet release.

Symbols dance in patterns faint,
Leading to a truth untaint.
A map unseen, a riddle deep,
The hidden puzzle does not sleep.

Solve the maze with heart and mind,
And to its secrets, you'll be kind.
The hidden puzzle, once unveiled,
Will tell a story long entailed.

Silhouettes of Doubt

In twilight's haze, where shadows blend,
Doubt's silhouettes begin and end.
A fragile form in moonlight traced,
Uncertainty's soft, ghostly embrace.

On paths uncharted, doubt does tread,
A silent whisper, in your head.
Shapes unclear in evening's light,
Doubt's silhouette, a haunting sight.

In every turn and every sigh,
The shadows shift, the questions pry.
Though doubt may darken, veil the view,
In clarity, the night renew.

Through veils of dusk and misted scenes,
Doubt's silhouette fades in between.
A lingering touch, a fleeting shade,
In doubt's embrace, the night is made.

Yet as the dawn breaks, shadows flee,
And doubt's silhouette no longer be.
In morning's light, truth finds its way,
Dispelling doubts of yesterday.

Mysterious Echoes

In the canyon's breath they linger
Whispers of a time untold
Voices blend with twilight's finger
Ancient stories to unfold

Silent ripples pierce the stillness
Hissed by winds from yesteryears
Ethereal on strings of illness
Sown with whispers' fervent tears

Wonders mystic, shrouds deceive
Breathless curses through the veil
Mysteries in echoes weave
Binding destinies with frail

Caverns deep with shadows play
Midnight tales to haunt the mind
Lurking secrets on display
Silent echoes left behind

Fleeting calls to those who listen
Hints and murmurs intertwined
Under star glow secrets glisten
Footprints of the spectral kind

Vanishing Traces

Footprints fade upon the sand
Gone before the tide reclaims
Vanishing into the land
Echoes whisper ancient names

Soft without a line of page
History in dust arrays
Time's own grand, unspoken stage
Traces lost in twilight's haze

Wanderers with fleeting past
Ciphers in the wind, they fly
Nothing holds a shadow cast
Stars alone bear final sigh

Paths dissolve where dreams converge
Fleeting steps dissolve from sight
Poignant is the murky purge
Held within the chasms tight

Veiled is dawn by mist and dew
Loss unheld, yet ever near
Eras fade, as ghosts construe
In the quiet disappear

Puzzles in the Shadows

Dustings of enigmas weave
Between the dark and softest light
Clues encased within believe
Silent symbols out of sight

Labyrinths of hidden sorrow
Draped in cryptic midnight's gleam
Where the night from day does borrow
Whispers form a fleeting dream

Puzzles etched on walls of gray
Secrets lock in shadow's grip
Truths obscure and thoughts astray
Parallel the mirrored slip

Differences in shadow's touch
Silent words and riddles dance
What reveals by moon is much
Light and dark's uncanny trance

Spectrum split with lines bemuse
Puzzles docker beams in glance
Shadows secrets they diffuse
Wrapped within the starry expanse

Secrets in the Dark

In the stillness of the night
Hidden truths with shadows play
Tales unseen by candlelight
Secrets in the dark convey

Silent verses written deep
In the heart of moonlit air
Darkness guarded, vows to keep
Whispers float with muted care

Veiled by night's embracing shroud
Hidden realms of old persist
In the darkness thoughts avowed
Silent longings, shadows twist

Words unspoken haunt the void
In the depths of night confide
Secrets in the dark deployed
Truths that hope and fears divide

In the quiet shadows loom
Guardians of unchecked lore
Secrets tender in the gloom
Eclipsed by moon's silent chore

Hidden Symphonies

In quiet glades where whispers flow,
Soft symphonies the breezes sow,
Unseen fingers pluck the air,
With melodies beyond compare.

Leaves rustle tunes in twilight hue,
While stars compose in skies so blue,
Nature's concert in disguise,
A masterpiece that never dies.

Beneath the moon's enchanting light,
Songs of shadows take their flight,
Each note a secret gently told,
In rhythms ancient, whispers old.

Listen close, the earth confides,
With harmonies the night provides,
A symphony hidden, pure and deep,
In every breath, the secrets keep.

Through the silence, hear it weave,
A song for hearts that dare believe,
In hidden symphonies so true,
Eternal, mute, yet ever new.

Shadowy Quests

In realms where sunlight softly fades,
Adventures mask in twilight shades,
Through forests dense and valleys low,
Where shadows dance and secrets flow.

Knights of dusk on quests unseen,
Ride through nightmares, silent, keen,
Their armor clad in ebony,
To claim their unseen destiny.

Through caverns dark and haunted caves,
Past ancient ruins and sunken graves,
They follow paths where shadows lead,
On quests dark fate and time decreed.

A whispered legend, faint and frail,
Speaks of heroes set to sail,
Through shadow's veil, their spirits quest,
Seeking solace, seeking rest.

In the end, what shall they find?
Truths mere shadows leave behind,
For in the darkness, light must quest,
To shadowy quests, the brave are blessed.

Ghostly Clues

In the stillness of the night,
Ghostly figures take their flight,
Whispers faint and shadows cast,
Clues from spirits of the past.

Footsteps echo, faint and clear,
Hidden messages they bear,
Histories within the gloom,
In ghostly clues, spirits loom.

Phantoms gliding through the air,
Secret hints they leave with care,
Haunting halls with tales untold,
Murmured secrets, ages old.

Candles flicker in the gloom,
Revealing truths within the room,
Spectral hands that guide the way,
Through ghostly clues to break of day.

Follow where the shadows lead,
Unveil the mysteries they seed,
In the dark, their whispers choose,
To give you strength with ghostly clues.

Echoing Voyages

Upon the waves, horizons gleam,
Sailors chase a distant dream,
Beyond the edge where oceans meet,
Echoing voyages, adventures greet.

The sea, a canvas vast and free,
Echoes tales of mystery,
Every crest and ocean's fold,
A story waiting to be told.

Through tempests wild and calm repose,
Where oceans whisper, skylines glow,
Echoes of the past align,
With new adventures intertwined.

Starry nights and moonlit skies,
Compass points and seagull's cries,
Echoes guide their hearts to rove,
In search of treasures tales behove.

Each wave an echo of the quest,
An odyssey that will not rest,
For voyagers, the sea will sing,
Of echoing voyages till the end of spring.

Codes of Forgotten Realms

In lands where ancient secrets lie,
Whispers of the past still breathe.
Elders' tales in code they wove,
Curtains drawn in hidden heave.

Symbols etched on weathered stone,
Mysteries clad in dusk's embrace.
Through twilight's veil we seek the keys,
Unraveling time, a sacred chase.

Wanderers from distant stars,
Navigate archaic streams.
Decrypt the lore, release the spells,
Awaken long-forgotten dreams.

Codex bound in twilight hues,
Pages speak in tongues unknown.
Guardians of the silent script,
Their vigilance forever sown.

In the heart of shadows cast,
Legends wait to be unbound.
Unearthing realms of ancient craft,
Where echoes of the lost resound.

Riddles in Moonlight

Moonlight spills on whispering leaves,
Mysteries in silver trace.
Dreams are spun in twilight's loom,
Riddles weave in mystic pace.

Stars align with cryptic lore,
Nebulas a map unseen.
Celestial queries flood the night,
In patterns vast, serene.

Forest paths by pale glow,
Guide us through enigma's gate.
Each shadow holds a whispered phrase,
Unraveling the night's debate.

Luminous reflections dance,
Across the surface of the pond.
Where whispers from the lunar plane,
Invoke a silence, calm yet fond.

Answers drift like evening mist,
Hints within the night air sown.
In the moon's soft, silent gaze,
Clues to secrets still unknown.

Hidden Trails

Through the woods where silence reigns,
Paths obscure and overgrown.
Step by step, the earth reveals,
Trails hidden, lightly shown.

Whispers of the ancient pines,
Guiding feet with gentle nudge.
In the shadows secrets seep,
Softly urging us to trudge.

Footprints lost in mossy beds,
Blend with roots and stones beneath.
Follow where the wild things tread,
In twilight's hazy wreath.

Creaking boughs speak softly now,
Of roads less traveled, veiled in green.
Nature hums its ancient tune,
Guide us to the unseen.

Beyond the bend, horizons merge,
Where the forest meets the sky.
On hidden trails we journey forth,
With the unknown as our guide.

Lost in Translation

Words dissolve in whispered air,
Meaning shifts on fleeting breeze.
Boundaries blur in tangled tongues,
Lost in cryptic entities.

Syntax binds but still it breaks,
Languages entwined, disperse.
Thoughts conveyed through broken lines,
Echoes trapped in universe.

In the space 'tween voice and ear,
Meaning wavers, left in haze.
Misunderstood yet softly clear,
Unseen paths in language maze.

Letters merge and letters part,
In the dance of silent speech.
We decipher, hearts align,
In the gaps, new worlds we reach.

Within the chaos, clarity,
Where the end and start emerge.
Bound by symbols, lost in text,
In this labyrinth, we converge.

Veiled Realities

In whispers of a twilight's breeze,
Secrets float like autumn leaves,
Shadows play where dreams convene,
In realms unseen, in realms unseen.

Mysteries wrapped in moonlight's lace,
Beyond this world's familiar face,
Ephemeral, a distant gleam,
In veiled realities we dream.

Each corner hides an untold tale,
As silence weaves its subtle veil,
Through gossamer of night's expanse,
We're led by fate and circumstance.

Light and dark both intertwine,
In patterns cryptic and divine,
Where truth lies cloaked in night's embrace,
Veiled realities we chase.

Yet in those depths, a wisdom lies,
Beyond the reach of worldly eyes,
In secrets known by dusk and dawn,
Veiled realities are drawn.

Phantom Evidence

Through corridors of ancient stone,
Echoes whisper, chilled and lone,
Ethereal, the truth we chase,
In phantom places we embrace.

Faint imprints of a bygone time,
Trace the lines of cryptic rhyme,
Subtle hints that ghosts bestow,
In phantom evidence we know.

Fleeting visions in the dark,
Leave behind a latent spark,
Clues that flicker in the night,
Phantom evidence in sight.

Haunted paths where shadows play,
Words unspoken softly sway,
Beneath the surface, stories seep,
In phantom evidence we keep.

Elusive threads that weave and wind,
Bind the realms of heart and mind,
In foggy mists, our thoughts they blend,
Phantom evidence, our friend.

Enigma's Lure

A riddle whispered in the breeze,
Pulls us through the ancient trees,
Unseen forces guide our quest,
Enigma's lure, we long to test.

Cryptic signs along the way,
Challenge us by night and day,
Paths that twist and turn anew,
Enigma's lure pulls us through.

Pondering along the shore,
Questions echo, more and more,
In the depths of twilight's blur,
We feel the pull of enigma's lure.

Lost in thoughts that never cease,
Seeking out a hidden peace,
Moments filled with silent clues,
Enigma's lure, a subtle muse.

Drawn by mysteries profound,
Within their depths, our souls are bound,
In shadows cast, in light obscure,
We chase the trace of enigma's lure.

Puzzles in the Dark

In the silence of the night,
Where shadows cast a subtle light,
Figures dance in hidden parts,
We find puzzles in the dark.

Every step a cautious guess,
Through a realm of soft finesse,
Hints that sparkle, secrets stark,
Solve the puzzles in the dark.

Voices carried by the breeze,
Speak in ancient, cryptic keys,
Listen close and you embark,
On solving puzzles in the dark.

Whispers echo through the air,
Mysteries beyond compare,
Patterns form and then embark,
To align puzzles in the dark.

Such the path and such the quest,
To untangle and invest,
Into realms where thoughts do hark,
Completing puzzles in the dark.

Mystery's Mirage

In sands of time, where shadows play,
Dreams are born to fade away.
A lonely dune whispers night,
Stars dissemble truth in sight.

Mirage appears, an echo's call,
Drawing hearts to its enthrall.
Ephemeral as morning dew,
Its secrets hide, then bid adieu.

Winds of change, they softly blow,
Skeletons of myths below.
In desert's vast, a tale untold,
Gold of history, mysteries unfold.

Oasis shimmers, heaven's guise,
Truth obscured in moonlit skies.
Journey forth on paths unknown,
Seeking mirage, forever flown.

Cloaked Realities

Behind the veil, a world unseen,
Truths obscure and souls pristine.
In shadows cast by candle's flame,
Lives are drawn to mythic frame.

Masked in secrets, hearts concealed,
Emotions raw, yet not revealed.
Eyes that gaze but do not see,
Cloaked realities, wandering free.

Whispers drift on twilight's breeze,
Mysteries hidden amidst the trees.
Through the mist, a path unfolds,
Stories whispered, never told.

In twilight's heart, a fading hue,
Moments lost like morning dew.
Veils of time and woven lore,
Cloaked realities, forevermore.

Riddles of Silence

In quietude, a secret lies,
Words unspoken, hidden sighs.
Nature's whispers softly call,
Riddles linger in the pall.

Silence speaks in night's embrace,
Mysteries drift in open space.
Questions linger, answers hide,
Within the hush, where doubts reside.

Echoes of the past revere,
Truths concealed in shadows clear.
In the stillness, secrets scream,
Riddles wrapped in silent dream.

Time reveals its cryptic trail,
Wrapped in silence, woven frail.
The answers float on wings of air,
Riddles binding, secrets bare.

Beneath the Surface

Beneath the surface, shadows blend,
Secrets whispered, threads that mend.
In the depths where visions sleep,
Dreams are forged and secrets keep.

Through the veil of water clear,
Lies a world both far and near.
Truths emerge in slumbered grace,
Silent echoes, hidden place.

Waves that whisper tales untold,
Weaving myths in currents cold.
Depths of ocean, hearts confide,
Mysteries flow with the tide.

Beneath the surface, silence reigns,
Veins of truth in hidden plains.
Dive below where secrets gleam,
Reality fades to endless dream.

Unseen Footprints

In the silence of the morning dew,
Unseen footprints softly tread.
A path where dreams are few,
And whispered secrets are spread.

Each step an echo of the heart,
On trails where shadows meet.
Invisible, yet a vital part,
Of every journey's beat.

Through forests dense and valleys wide,
Unseen, but ever true.
These footprints mark the soul's stride,
In hues of calm and blue.

They blend with sun and moon's flight,
A dance of time unending.
Unseen footprints in the night,
Life and light amending.

So let us walk with gentle grace,
Leave marks where love abides.
In unseen footprints we embrace,
The path where spirit guides.

Unraveled Threads

In the loom of destiny's hand,
Threads of life are tightly spun.
Weave together across the land,
Until our stories are done.

Each strand a tale of joy and woe,
Interwoven with care.
Unraveled threads begin to show,
Secrets beyond compare.

The tapestry of dreams we weave,
Worn by time and tide.
Threads that break and strands that leave,
In patterns they reside.

Yet in the fray, we find our grace,
In every thread undone.
Mend the heart and hold the space,
For battles lost and won.

Unraveled threads, a life's embrace,
A fabric torn and bright.
In every stitch, a sacred place,
Of darkness turned to light.

Eclipsed Memories

Beneath the shadow of the moon,
Eclipsed memories unfold.
A silent, cosmic tune,
Of tales both young and old.

The past in shades of dusk,
Secrets softly intertwined.
Moments caught in a husk,
Of a time once so kind.

These memories in the dark,
Whisper of things unseen.
A single, fleeting spark,
In a world of might-have-been.

They linger in the twilight,
A dream that fades away.
Eclipsed beneath the night,
Where silent echoes play.

Yet in the quiet, we recall,
The beauty of the yore.
Eclipsed memories stand tall,
Silent sentinels of lore.

Mysterious Whispers

In the quiet of the night,
Mysterious whispers flow.
A soft, enchanting sight,
Where secrets come to know.

The wind, it tells a tale,
Of ages long and far.
In whispers, none too frail,
The world's a wishing star.

Between the shadows, light,
A murmur or a sigh.
Whispers beyond plain sight,
Where unseen truths lie.

Hushed tones that sway the soul,
A gentle, mystic breeze.
Whispers that make us whole,
In their tender pleas.

So listen to the night,
The mysteries it shares.
In whispers soft and bright,
We find our answers there.

The Obscure Path

In twilight's gentle, veiled disguise,
A pathway winds beneath unknown skies,
With each step forward, echoes fly,
Whispers of secrets gone awry.

Leaves stir softly in a phantom's breath,
Guiding souls through shadows' depth,
Moonlight peeks from clouds of gray,
Lighting the obscure path's way.

Bound by fate's unspoken thread,
We tread where angels fear to tread,
Each twist and turn, a riddle cast,
Forever forging, futures past.

Stars above in silent symphony,
Guide the steps to destiny,
In the darkness, dreams take flight,
Along the path of myth and night.

Amidst the still of nature's loom,
Answers found in shadowed gloom,
The obscure path, it calls to thee,
Walk with wonder, wild and free.

Perplexity Unveiled

Shadows cloak the night in mystery,
Veiling truths in history,
Caught within the swirling gale,
Comes perplexity unveiled.

In the labyrinth of time's embrace,
Questions dance in fleeting grace,
Through the fog of thoughts entwined,
Clarity, we seek to find.

Eyes that wander into night,
Gaze upon uncertain sights,
From the dark, a beacon flares,
Perplexity with secrets bares.

Through the haze of doubt and dream,
Nothing's ever as it seems,
Unraveling the hidden tale,
Perplexity is soon unveiled.

In the silence, whispers fade,
Revelations gently made,
With each step, the truth avails,
Perplexity, at last, unveiled.

The Forgotten Map

Through dusty shelves and faded lore,
Lies a tale from days of yore,
Of a map forgotten, hid away,
In the shadows bleak and gray.

Ancient lines on parchment frail,
Speak of lands beyond the vale,
Marked by time and whispers lost,
It bears the stories tempest-tossed.

Travelers seek with hearts afire,
Driven by a deep desire,
To uncover paths concealed,
Where the map has been revealed.

Winds of change and errant flights,
Carry dreams on moonlit nights,
Guided by the stars on high,
Chasing echoes of a sigh.

In the end, one finds the key,
Unlocking realms of mystery,
The forgotten map guides true,
To wonders old and new.

The Disappearing Act

Beneath the stage lights' dimming glow,
Where shadows dance and secrets flow,
A world of dreams, both wild and mild,
Awaits within the mysteries styled.

A flick of wrist, a cape of black,
Illusions form, then slip to track,
Vanishing in a blink of sight,
The disappearing act takes flight.

Silence falls as whispers rise,
Magic woven through the skies,
In the cloak of night's dark seam,
Reality blurs into a dream.

Masters of the unseen art,
Crafting realms that spark the heart,
In the hush of breathless pact,
Lies the soul of the act.

Ephemeral as the morning mist,
Fading out to sun's sweet kiss,
The disappearing act holds sway,
Enchants the night, then slips away.

Midnight's Conundrum

In silence where the shadows play,
Across the moonlit path they stray,
A riddle whispers through the trees,
With answers carried on the breeze.

Stars like secrets in the night,
Guide the wanderers to the light,
Yet in the dark, the doubts they breed,
What is it that our hearts most need?

The clock ticks softly on the wall,
Midnight holds us in its thrall,
A question echoes in our mind,
Is truth or dream what we will find?

Ghostly whispers, soft and clear,
Haunt the midnight atmosphere,
In the conundrum of the dark,
The soul ignites its seeking spark.

Where lies the key to twilight's door?
In dreams it whispers evermore,
The answer hidden deep within,
The midnight conundrum shall begin.

The Locked Box

A box sits there with secrets kept,
Within its heart, old promises slept,
Bound tightly by a rusted key,
What wonders might we someday see?

In darkness, it remains concealed,
With mysteries that time revealed,
Each layer hides a tale untold,
Each hinge is touched by faded gold.

Curiosity's unyielding force,
The mind begins its silent course,
To find the truth in hidden locks,
Within the heart of this old box.

Ancient whispers call our name,
In quiet dreams, we play the game,
Of unlocking history's veil,
And letting loose the secret tale.

Once the box is open wide,
And truths no longer have to hide,
We'll understand what time had sealed,
In the locked box, now revealed.

Unseen Winds

The winds of change are never seen,
They move through life on paths unseen,
Invisible yet full of might,
They guide us gently through the night.

With whispers soft, they touch our face,
And move with ever-changing grace,
They herald storms and skies so clear,
The unseen winds that we all hear.

They carry scents from distant shores,
And open wide unseen doors,
Their dance is felt on skin and leaf,
A silent witness to belief.

In autumn's fall, in winter's chill,
In spring's soft touch, they linger still,
And summer's breath they soon embrace,
In unseen winds, we find our place.

Though we may never see their form,
They guide us through life's fleeting storm,
For in the winds, a truth does sing,
Invisible, yet everything.

Tales Without End

Stories told by candlelight,
In the quiet of the night,
We weave the past with threads so fine,
In tales that intertwine.

From ancient lands to future dreams,
Where nothing's ever as it seems,
Each word a bridge from then to when,
We tell these tales again.

Heroes rise and monsters fall,
Through every realm and every hall,
With love and courage, battles fend,
In stories with no end.

From whispered myths to epic lore,
In every heart, a tale is stored,
A legacy of times we've penned,
In tales without an end.

So gather 'round and listen close,
To tales where endless magic flows,
For in each story, life extends,
In tales that never end.

Concealed Signs

Beneath the surface, shadows play
Whispers of time, just slip away
In ancient runes, secrets reside
Encrypted whispers, never to hide

A dance of light, a silent gaze
Ambient tales in dusky haze
Hints in twilight, elusive and fine
The universe speaks, through concealed signs

In the breeze, through branches thin
There lie messages, hidden within
An unsolved puzzle, a cosmic rhyme
Silent yet loud, across space and time

Mirrors reflect what eyes can't see
A realm of truth, in mystery
Engraved in stars, in sacred designs
The world unfolds, through concealed signs

In shadows deep, and echoes faint
Lie truths, wrapped in a subtle taint
The silent cosmos, ever it aligns
Reveals its heart, through concealed signs

Veiled Mysteries

In the shroud of night, secrets sleep
Guardians of tales, shadows keep
Under the moon's soft, silken glow
Veiled mysteries, begin to flow

Stars whispering ancient lore
Silent echoes from ages yore
Celestial bodies, a cryptic spree
Veiled mysteries, they long to be

Whispers of the wind through the trees
Hidden truths on a twilight breeze
Beyond the horizon's velvet mist
Veiled mysteries, persist, insist

The dance of shadows, the cloak of night
Concealing wisdom, banished from sight
In the depths of time, in cosmic seas
Lie everlasting veiled mysteries

Through lifetimes they hide, truths so vast
Fragments of future, pieces of past
In every secret, a silent plea
Unlock the tales, of veiled mystery

Echoes of Obscurity

In the corners where light rarely treads
Dwells the realm where the echoes spread
Unfound whispers of ages old
In obscurity, stories are cold

The subtle hum of long-lost time
An ancient's breath in silent rhyme
In the void where memories seep
Echoes of obscurity, forever keep

In shadows cast by forgotten lore
Faint murmurs from an unseen shore
Invisible threads weave silent ties
Echoes of obscurity, where silence lies

Through nights so deep, without a cast
Sings a chorus from eons past
In the stillness, a ceaseless plea
These echoes of obscurity

In silent depths, where secrets thrive
An ancient song, forever alive
In whispers hushed, profoundly free
Dwell echoes of obscurity

Arcane Silhouettes

Beneath the moon's ephemeral light
Shapes of wonder dance in sight
Forms of legends, shadows beget
Otherworldly arcane silhouettes

In twilight's grasp, they come alive
Ancient beings continue to thrive
In their dance, forgotten regrets
Are rekindled, by arcane silhouettes

Mystique forms in a liquid dance
Through the void, they twist, they prance
Etched in time, in starlit nets
Frame the night, these arcane silhouettes

Outlines of dreams and silent fears
Page of history, soaked in tears
In their wake, the night begets
Mysterious arcane silhouettes

As dawn splits night with golden flame
They melt away, from whence they came
Leaving behind, a tale beset
Whispered only, by arcane silhouettes

The Quiet Paradox

In quiet, we find the loudest cries,
In stillness, worlds within us rise.
Peaceful realms of paradox,
Silent screams behind closed locks.

Mountains whisper ancient lore,
In shadows, light forevermore.
Paths converge in hidden glades,
Mysteries, both light and shade.

Timeless tales in silence spun,
Stars entwine, their dance begun.
Midst the hush, a heart's loud beat,
Silent thunders, bittersweet.

Wisdom wears a quiet cloak,
Truth, a muted anthem spoke.
Paradox in every turn,
Silent fires forever burn.

Eloquent in muted tone,
Secrets in the silence sown.
Paradox, our hidden guide,
In quiet, truths do long reside.

Intrigues of Silence

Soft sections of the silent night,
Stories in the quiet light.
Echoes of the thoughts we hide,
Whispering winds, they softly bide.

In the hush, the heart discerns,
Mysteries which nature spurns.
Every quiet breath we take,
Intrigues spun, intentions fake.

Through the void, connections spark,
Quiet truths in hidden dark.
Soundless tales of endless lore,
Silent waves upon the shore.

Unseen strings of fate entwine,
Silent clocks that mark our time.
Ethereal sighs, elusive fate,
Silence holds our cryptic gate.

Intrigues swirl in soundless halls,
Whispered echoes, ancient calls.
Beneath the still, the secrets keep,
In silence, truths forever sleep.

Glimpses of the Enigmatic

In shadows, light begins to dance,
From the mist, a fleeting glance.
Nebulous realms within our sight,
Glimpses of the enigmatic night.

Mystery dons a quiet veil,
In the void, we trace a trail.
Whispers of the cosmic rhyme,
Moments caught in space and time.

Secrets cast in twilight's hue,
Hidden worlds and vistas new.
Each blink a portal to the known,
Fleeting glimpses, magic shown.

Ephemeral as the morning dew,
Timeless truths we glimpse and skew.
Veiled midst the woven thread,
Enigmas live where dreams have fled.

Glimpses spark imagination, bright,
In dawn's or dimming, failing light.
The vague becomes the panoramic,
Glimpses of the enigmatic.

The Vanishing Point

Horizons blend in misty hues,
Where sky meets earth, a hidden ruse.
In the distance, truths align,
Vanishing points through space and time.

Lines converge, yet drift apart,
In the fade, the secrets start.
Parallel paths in fading light,
Merging realms beyond our sight.

The closer we approach, they flee,
Chasing whispers, endlessly.
Vanishing with every breath,
Distance masking depth and breadth.

Visions fade and reappear,
Ephemeral and ever near.
Elusive as the dying day,
Vanishing points, they slip away.

Contours blurred from dark to light,
Merging shades of day and night.
In the end, all paths unite,
At the vanishing point of sight.

Milton Keynes UK
Ingram Content Group UK Ltd.
UKHW011648130624
444169UK00015B/221